CW00972233

A Journey wi

A Holy Week Bible Study

David Thomson

Authentic
LIFESTYLE

Copyright © 2004 David Thomson, and the original copyright holders

First published 2004 by Authentic Lifestyle

Authentic Lifestyle is an imprint of Authentic Media,
P.O. Box 300, Carlisle, Cumbria, CA3 0QS, U.K.
and
P.O. Box 1047, Waynesboro, GA 30830-2047, U.S.A.

10 09 08 07 06 05 04   7 6 5 4 3 2 1

The right of David Thomson to be identified as the Author of this Work has been asserted
by him in accordance with the Copyright, Designs and Patents Act 1988.

*All rights reserved. No part of this publication may be reproduced, stored in a retrieval system,
or transmitted in any form or by any means, electric, mechanical, photocopying, recording or
otherwise, without the prior permission of the publisher or a licence permitting restricted
copying. In the U.K. such licences are issued by the Copyright Licensing Agency,
90, Tottenham Court Road, London W1P 9HE.*

British Library Cataloguing in Publication Data
A catalogue record for this book is available from the British Library

ISBN 1-85078-561-9

Unless otherwise stated, Scripture quotations are taken from the
HOLY BIBLE, NEW INTERNATIONAL VERSION
Copyright © 1973, 1978, 1984 by the International Bible Society.
Used by permission of Hodder and Stoughton Limited. All rights reserved.
'NIV' is a registered trademark of the International Bible Society
UK trademark number 1448790.

Designed and typeset by Christopher Lawther, Teamwork, Lancing, West Sussex.
Produced by Jeremy Mudditt Publishing Services, Carlisle,
and printed and bound in Great Britain by Dualcrest Printers, Lancing, West Sussex.

CONTENTS

ABOUT THIS BOOK

How to use the book

How can we move from Lent to Easter in a way that will really develop our approach to the passion of Christ and the joy of his resurrection? The week immediately before Easter is traditionally called 'Holy Week' and it is an ideal time to dig deeper into the passion narratives of the gospels, and let them bear in on our own lives.

This booklet offers you the opportunity to take a Holy Week journey with St John along the way of Jesus' Passion. Part of the gospel is printed out each day for you to read, followed by a meditation in five or so sections, each with a pointed question to help you deepen your understanding of what Jesus' sacrifice can mean for you today. A prayer ends the day's study – hopefully a starter for your own prayers. You'll also find some 'extras' in boxes here and there to help you take your time and address your own feelings during this Passiontide journey.

Using the book in a group

We are used to weekly study groups and Lent groups. Why not set up a Holy Week group, meeting for an hour at lunchtime, after you drop the children off at school, or after work?

You could light a candle and say an opening prayer, before asking one of the group to read the passage for the day out loud. Then group members can take turns in reading the paragraphs which follow, giving space after each not for discussion but for other group members to add a thought or a comment. (It is an important rule not to comment on each other's comments!) Finally, the set prayer could be read and open prayer follow for as long as you have time.

Saturday as a day of waiting and preparation

There is no study set for Saturday! Equally the Gospels are silent at this point.

Holy Saturday is a day for quiet waiting, for allowing ourselves to let go of the busy-ness of religion and simply *be* before the mystery of the Living God who is in the tomb.

Your group meeting or quiet time can best be just that – a time of silence before the noisy joy of Easter.

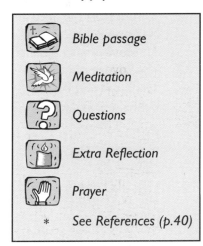

	Bible passage
	Meditation
	Questions
	Extra Reflection
	Prayer
*	See References (p.40)

Arrival: A Matter of Life and Death?

Today's Bible passage

Six days before the Passover, Jesus arrived at Bethany, where Lazarus lived, whom Jesus had raised from the dead. Here a dinner was given in Jesus' honour. Martha served, while Lazarus was among those reclining at the table with him. Then Mary took about a pint of pure nard, an expensive perfume; she poured it on Jesus' feet and wiped his feet with her hair. And the house was filled with the fragrance of the perfume.

But one of his disciples, Judas Iscariot, who was later to betray him, objected, 'Why wasn't this perfume sold and the money given to the poor? It was worth a year's wages.' He did not say this because he cared about the poor but because he was a thief; as keeper of the money bag, he used to help himself to what was put into it.

'Leave her alone,' Jesus replied. 'It was intended that she should save this perfume for the day of my burial. You will always have the poor among you, but you will not always have me.'

Meanwhile a large crowd of Jews found out that Jesus was there and came, not only because of him but also to see Lazarus, whom he had raised from the dead. So the chief priests made plans to kill Lazarus as well, for on account of him many of the Jews were going over to Jesus and putting their faith in him.

JOHN 12.1-11

The Flight of the Eagle

Listen! Look! The eagle is hovering now at the full height of its climb, watching, waiting, ready to begin its triumphant stoop and ascent, from glory to glory.

As we start our journey with John, it's good to remember that each of the gospel writers has their own

style, their own approach. We don't just have four clones of one book, but the insights and personal faith of four very different men.

Mark is reportage, sound bites and short clips. Matthew is a teacher's book about the greatest teacher of all, the new Moses. Luke writes history, all gathered in order, to set the record straight.

John is poetry, drama, more film than discourse. There are fewer scenes, but they are more vivid. His waters run deep with symbolism – a gospel, according to an ancient saying, in which a child can paddle but an elephant swim*. We see the events, but we also see into the characters; we see what is happening, but we also see why.

And John's Jesus is like the eagle which is used to symbolise his gospel. He comes from heaven to heaven, descending and ascending, from glory to glory. He knows exactly what he is about, and here, at the beginning of chapter 12, he has gained the full height of his ministry, raising Lazarus from the dead – the miracle of miracles, reported only by John, and completely characteristic of John, who speaks of salvation as simply *life*. 'I have come that they may have life, and have it to the full,' says John's Jesus, and it draws us to him.

QUESTION

Close your eyes for a moment!
What is your picture of Jesus?

A Matter of Life and Death

This second part of John's Gospel is a matter of life and death, for Jesus, for those who are around him, and for us now. The raising of Lazarus is the zenith of Jesus' ministry, but also the point from which he must fall, down, down to certain death, only to rise up again triumphant, so that even the cross itself is bathed in glory.

So the clock now starts its countdown: six days to the Passover – the Passover which for John is not the Thursday supper but the sacrifice of Jesus, the Lamb of God, on the Friday.

Our scene opens with Jesus at dinner with Lazarus. It was a dinner among friends. Bethany must have been Jesus' regular base when visiting Jerusalem, which lies only a couple of miles to the west. He knew Mary well, but while he may have expected the unexpected, the rest of the company was shocked to the core by what she did then. The perfume would have been worth a cool two thousand pounds at today's prices: an heirloom product, sealed into its alabaster flask; and its fragrance filled the air.

The anointing speaks of the grave, but also of kingship. John sets this scene before, not after, the entry into Jerusalem; and remember that for him even the cross is the throne.

QUESTION

Try entering the scene of the anointing in your imagination. How do you find yourself reacting?

A Passion for You

CPO, Worthing

The silence is broken abruptly by Judas. There is no hiding his character here. The text names him as a betrayer from the beginning, and his face and voice will speak his character. He may be in a place of honour, the keeper of the money bag, the distributor of charity, but John uses a word for 'keep' that means 'lift', and which could mean to steal as much then as it could now.

Jesus' response is as abrupt as Judas' intervention. The grammar of his Greek breaks down. The tone feels like something out of *cinéma noir*: 'This is something between the lady and me.' The feel is sensual, heavy with perfume and implication. A respectable woman of the time would have no more let down her hair in public to wipe someone's feet than a lady now would take off her blouse to mop a guest's brow.

I wonder how you feel about a Jesus like this. It's not a very 'British' moment; but John's Gospel has love at its heart, and it will stretch and challenge the boundaries of our behaviour. This is the Gospel that speaks of God so loving the world, of Jesus showing the full extent of his love, of the new commandment to love one another, of the greater love that lays down its life, of the love that Peter must declare to find restitution.

QUESTION

Is it disconcerting for you to think of Jesus as passionate? Does it make his Passion more or less relevant to you?

Love's Expense

Each of the readings this week says something important about love, and this reading now speaks of love's necessary generosity, even extravagance.

'O generous love! that he who smote in man for man the foe, the double agony in man for man should undergo.' (from Cardinal Newman's hymn *Praise to the Holiest in the Height**.)

True love detests limits: it does not measure itself but pours itself out, to the point where it is vulnerable and out of control. It is not constrained by expectation or convention, but creates its own truth. It shatters the ceiling of its credit limit not because it is worth it, but because of the worth of the beloved.

Morning glory, starlit sky,
Soaring music, scholars' truth,
Flight of swallows, autumn leaves,
Memory's treasure, grace of youth:

Open are the gifts of God,
Gifts of love to mind and sense;
Hidden is love's agony,
Love's endeavour, love's expense.

Love that gives, gives ever more,
Gives with zeal, with eager hands,
Spares not, keeps not, all outpours,
Ventures all, its all expends.

Drained is love in making full,
Bound in setting others free,
Poor in making many rich,
Weak in giving power to be.

Therefore he who shows us God
Helpless hangs upon the tree;
And the nails and crown of thorns
Tell of what God's love must be.

Here is God: no monarch he,
Throned in easy state to reign;
Here is God, whose arms of love
Aching, spent, the world sustain.

W. H. Vanstone*

Contrast what the Irish poet John Boyle O'Reilly described as 'The organized charity, scrimped and iced, in the name of a cautious, statistical Christ*' with the life of someone like Mother Teresa. In her own words, 'Faith cannot be genuine without being generous. Love and Faith go together; they complement each other.'

I heard recently of a man called Bob Thompson* – no relation – who built a successful business from scratch. The business thrived and he retired a wealthy man. He sold the company for an enormous amount of money. Then he stunned his former employees by giving them extravagant shares of the proceeds. Eighty of them became instant millionaires. All he could say was: 'It was the right thing to do.'

What about us? We are dealing with deep but real things here. We can sense very quickly, intuitively, whether another is a taker from life, or a giver of and to it; whether they are fundamentally closed and defended, or open and vulnerable.

QUESTION

What about us? What have we given, are we giving — at the moment, in the recent past? Does generosity come naturally to us, or do we count out our love?

Amazing Grace

And if it is hard to be generous, it is often even harder to receive generosity. At first that sounds quite upside-down. But stay with the thought a little longer. What are your feelings when another showers presents on you, treats you, shows you undeserved honour and respect? Humility seems to demand that we demur: but a deeper humility knows how to receive as well as to give.

When I was teaching in Oxford, I had several Japanese students, who seemed to love learning Old English. I could only admire their linguistic skills! What struck me even more, though, was the incredible generosity that they took for granted in the pupil-teacher relationship. Yasuhiro would throw the most wonderful supper parties, gave me presents that I still treasure today, and left my Yorkshire parsimony speechless.

Then as a minister, especially when I was working on a housing estate with desperate social problems, a bereaved family would press a gift on me that I knew they could ill afford. I would try to give it back, but their eyes said that that would be to deny

Japanese hospitality

their love. I would try to turn it into a gift to the church, but no it was for me. I had to learn again the language of love.

Undeserved love, extravagant love is at the very heart of our faith. While we are yet sinners, God loves us. He pours himself out for us. For him it is a matter of life and death.

For us too it is a matter of life and death.

Sometimes, Lord, I feel poured out too.
Demands press in on me from every side.
I hardly have a minute to call my own.
My own?
Yes, Lord – forgive me.
I still count what I keep as gain
And what I give away as loss.
I still patrol the boundary of my self
Watching warily for anything
That will threaten me.
And yet, I know it's true.
The more I give, the more I receive.
The more I lock the doors of my life,
The more I die.
It's scary, Lord – but now,
At the beginning of this Holy Week,
I want to take the risk
- the risk of faith.
I want to open my life, Lord, to yours.
Amen.

Thanks be to Thee, my Lord Jesus Christ,
For all the benefits
Which Thou hast won for me;
For all the pains and insults
Which Thou hast borne for me.
O Most Merciful Redeemer,
Friend and Brother;
May I know Thee more clearly,
Love Thee more dearly,
And follow Thee more nearly,
Day by day.
Amen.

ST RICHARD OF CHICHESTER *

Encounters: Death or Glory?

Today's Bible passage

There were some Greeks among those who went up to Jerusalem to worship at the Feast of the Passover. They came to Philip, who was from Bethsaida in Galilee, with a request. 'Sir,' they said, 'we would like to see Jesus.' Philip went to tell Andrew; Andrew and Philip in turn told Jesus.

Jesus replied, 'The hour has come for the Son of Man to be glorified. I tell you the truth, unless a grain of wheat falls to the ground and dies, it remains only a single seed. But if it dies, it produces many seeds. The man who loves his life will lose it, while the man who hates his life in this world will keep it for eternal life. Whoever serves me must follow me; and where I am, my servant also will be. My Father will honour the one who serves me.

'Now my heart is troubled, and what shall I say? "Father, save me from this hour"? No, it was for this very reason I came to this hour. Father, glorify your name!'

Then a voice came from heaven, 'I have glorified it, and will glorify it again.' The crowd that was there and heard it said it had thundered; others said an angel had spoken to him.

Jesus said, 'This voice was for your benefit, not mine. Now is the time for judgment on this world; now the prince of this world will be driven out. But I, when I am lifted up from the earth, will draw all men to myself.' He said this to show the kind of death he was going to die.

The crowd spoke up, 'We have heard from the Law that the Christ will remain for ever, so how can you say, "The Son of Man must be lifted up"? Who is this "Son of Man"?'

Then Jesus told them, 'You are going to have the light just a little while longer. Walk while you have the light, before darkness overtakes you. The man who walks in the dark does not know where he is going. Put your trust in the light while you have it, so that you may become sons of light.' When he had finished speaking, Jesus left and hid himself from them.

JOHN 12.20-36

Tourists or Pilgrims?

'The whole world has gone after him,' say the Pharisees in the verse before today's reading begins. The whole world seemed to converge on Jerusalem at Passover time. One census counted more than a quarter of a million lambs sacrificed there at one Passover: two and a half million people sharing Passover meals. (If we are to believe Josephus*, who is not always easy to believe!)

This was a pilgrim festival, but also something of a tourist attraction too, and the great tourists of the ancient world were the Greeks. They were notorious for chasing after novelty. As the writer of Acts put it, 'All the Athenians spent their time doing nothing but talking about and listening to the latest ideas.'

The scene, then, is the bustling Temple Courtyard, to which many came to worship and more to stare. The light is perhaps fading – Jesus seems to use that as an image a little later – but people still linger. Some Greeks see their opportunity to meet Jesus, to get his autograph as it were. I imagine them overhearing Philip – a man with a Greek name from a Greek-speaking town – and latching on to him. The shot tracks from the Greeks to Philip, to Andrew, and on to Jesus: replaying in reverse the sequence at the beginning of the Gospel.

The camera never moves back to the Greeks. They fade out completely from the story and are not heard of again. They have served their purpose for John: a sign that indeed all the world was now coming to Jesus, and that the time was right for the final act to begin. The encounter that matters is not theirs with Jesus, but Jesus' with the devil and death on Good Friday; and that encounter begins now.

QUESTION

I have called this day's study 'Encounters'. How serious an encounter are you ready to have with Christ? Are you a tourist or a pilgrim?

Death and Glory

'The hour has come,' says Jesus, 'for the Son of Man to be glorified.' These resounding words will ring out three times before they are fulfilled on the cross: here, after Judas leaves, and in the great prayer Jesus offers before leaving for Gethsemane. Our Lord is now completely focussed on the sacrifice of Calvary. 'Unless a grain of wheat falls to the ground and dies, it remains only a single seed. But if it dies, it produces many seeds.'

It is now that John's Jesus encounters his Gethsemane moment. 'Now my heart is troubled, and what shall I say? "Father, save me from this hour"? No, it was for this very reason that I came to this hour. Father, glorify your name!' There is no agony here. For John it is not death *or* glory but death *and* glory. So Gethsemane gives way immediately to what we can also call John's Transfiguration. 'Then a voice came from heaven, "I have glorified it, and will glorify it again."' If it were not the Gospel it would be pure theatre. But it is the Gospel, and it is meant for real.

The voice roars out like thunder – not an uncommon thing at that time of year in Judaea as I know to my cost, after promising a party I led there good weather! But the important thing about the roar is the responses it evokes. Like Aslan's roar in the Narnia books, it lends strength to the believer, but strikes fear and confusion into his enemies. Here the voice of God, silent for so long according to the Rabbis, speaks at last – but for many it goes unrecognised, even though it was for their benefit, just as many will pass the sacrifice on the cross by too.

The note is triumphant, and John's Jesus often does seem to walk a centimetre or two off the ground. But we must not be misled into thinking that the cross is anything other than an instrument of torture and death. The victory of Christ is not that he walks over it, but *through* it. It will be as much a losing of life for him as for us, and it is only sure faith in what lies beyond that makes the difference.

QUESTION

Most of us are culturally distant from a real sense of powerful kingship. Spend a moment pondering the power and kingship of Christ.

Not only the Gospel but our Lives

We thought yesterday about the generosity, even extravagance of love. It is possible, if you are rich enough, to give costly gifts, but at little real cost. Love requires sacrifice. Love is a giving of ourselves as well as our goods. I recently heard the minister of a church on a housing estate speak at a prayer meeting about how he had been challenged to give to that place in a way that put himself on the line. Words from Paul's letter to the Thessalonians had challenged him to the core: 'We loved you so much that we were delighted to share with you not only the gospel of God but our lives as well, because you had become so dear to us.' Not only the gospel, but our lives as well.

Or perhaps you remember those dreadful months a few years ago in America when first adults and then even children took guns into their local schools and brought into sickening reality the slaughter of the computer screen game. A teacher, Shannon Wright, acted instinctively when she saw one of the attackers aim at a 12-year-old girl in her class. Jumping in front of her, she took the bullets meant for the child and suffered mortal wounds to the chest and abdomen. The young girl whom she saved said, 'I think Mrs. Wright saw those bullets coming. She grabbed me by the shoulders and pushed me out of the way. She never thought of herself, just the children.*'

Such a calling does not require us to be rich or influential. Let me give you an illustration. We often light candles in church. Their purpose may once have been practical: it has always been symbolic. The pale, waxy candle has the look and feel of death. Only as it gives itself away through the furnace of the flame does it speak of life. From the candle's point of view it is only sacrifice: it will be used up, spent. But beyond its imagining, if we can allow it for a moment a soul, there is light and life for others of a completely new order. See too how even a small flame can conquer an enormity of darkness. Its death is its glory.

QUESTION

What person or situation is God calling you towards that may involve self-giving sacrifice?

Loving our Enemies

There have been people in all ages who have paid the full price of love. St Alphege was Archbishop of Canterbury in the early eleventh century, when the Danes were over-running south-east England*. Already famous for his austere lifestyle and lavish almsgiving, when he was held to ransom by the Danes for the enormous sum of £3000 he forbad anyone to pay, lest they became yet further impoverished, and he was murdered by his captors.

Elizabeth of Hungary lost her husband to the plague in the 1220's*. While he was alive she gave the palace's corn reserves to feed the poor, and housed many sick in rooms beneath the castle, visiting them daily and selling her own jewels to meet their needs. There were many children there who called her 'mother', and she would take even those with the worst diseases into her arms. Eventually the strictness of her life so weakened her that she herself died.

© Dean and Chapter of Westminster

Edith Cavell was a nurse serving in Belgium in the first World War*. After helping the sick on both sides she also began to help British prisoners escape, and was herself caught and shot, forgiving her executioners.

Janani Luwum was Archbishop of Uganda under Idi Amin's regime*. He was murdered on Amin's orders after he protested against the state violence that was becoming endemic there. Even when it was clear that he was *persona non grata* Luwum continued to attend government functions, saying that, 'Even the President needs friends. We must love the President. We must pray for him. He is a child of God.'

Janani Luwum

QUESTION

Who do you find hard to love?
What can you do about that?

Costly Presence

But what does costly love mean to us as we measure out our lives with coffee spoons, far removed from such drama? Let me suggest a simple rule we can follow. If we want to present ourselves to God, in the words of the old 1662 Book of Common Prayer, as 'a reasonable, holy and lively sacrifice unto thee', we must practise being wholly present to him – and to our neighbours – first. *Wholly* with a 'W' and an 'H'.

The devil is in the detail. There is all the difference in the world between giving a lot, and giving all. I go away for quiet days and retreats regularly. In a week given in one sense entirely over to God, I am doing well if just one minute is spent being wholly present to him, wholly in his presence. But that minute is the one that matters.

How present are you now, to God, to the person next to you? How present will you be to the people you go home to or meet tomorrow? How present will you be when someone next needs your aid?

It's not fair, Lord.
I open the door an inch,
And you want to come right in
And take over the whole house.
My house.
My castle.
My retreat.
Can't you be a decent guest
And just sit where I put you,
Make polite conversation
And go before I get too tired?
Help me, Lord.
This is holy ground.
I do want to be at one, as one,
  with you.
I do know that in you is my
  word of life.
Just help me
To ease the hinges of my heart.
Amen.

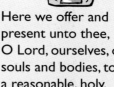

Here we offer and present unto thee, O Lord, ourselves, our souls and bodies, to be a reasonable, holy, and lively sacrifice unto thee; humbly beseeching thee, that all we, who are partakers of this holy Communion, may be fulfilled with thy grace and heavenly benediction.

BOOK OF COMMON PRAYER
Post Communion Prayer

Almighty God,
unto whom all hearts be open,
all desires known,
and from whom no secrets are hid:
cleanse the thoughts of our hearts
by the inspiration of thy Holy Spirit,
that we may perfectly love thee,
and worthily magnify thy holy name;
through Christ our Lord.
Amen.

BOOK OF COMMON PRAYER
Collect for Purity, at Holy Communion

Today's Bible passage

Jesus was troubled in spirit and testified, 'I tell you the truth, one of you is going to betray me.'

His disciples stared at one another, at a loss to know which of them he meant. One of them, the disciple whom Jesus loved, was reclining next to him. Simon Peter motioned to this disciple and said, 'Ask him which one he means.'

Leaning back against Jesus, he asked him, 'Lord, who is it?'

Jesus answered, 'It is the one to whom I will give this piece of bread when I have dipped it in the dish.' Then, dipping the piece of bread, he gave it to Judas Iscariot, son of Simon. As soon as Judas took the bread, Satan entered into him.

'What you are about to do, do quickly,' Jesus told him, but no-one at the meal understood why Jesus said this to him. Since Judas had charge of the money, some thought Jesus was telling him to buy what was needed for the Feast, or to give something to the poor. As soon as Judas had taken the bread, he went out. And it was night.

When he was gone, Jesus said, 'Now is the Son of Man glorified and God is glorified in him. If God is glorified in him, God will glorify the Son in himself, and will glorify him at once.'

JOHN 13.21-32

One of You ...

Yesterday it seemed that nothing could touch Jesus. Even the cross to come was turned to glory. I said then that we should not be misled, and today we see why. The sacrifice of the cross was something Jesus seemed to take in his stride: it was after all the clear will of his Father; it was why he came. But his betrayal by a friend is something else. 'Jesus was troubled in spirit and testified, "I tell you the truth, one of you is going to betray me."'

To feel the full impact of the situation we need to understand the seating plan at the Last Supper. We can imagine John's camera-like eye tracking round the room. The party are reclining on couches set at an angle to the table, head inwards obviously enough, leaning on their left sides and with their feet stretching back to the right. Each head is close to the chest of the man on the left.

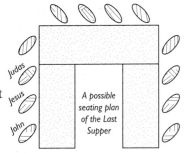

A possible seating plan of the Last Supper

Jesus' outburst stuns his companions. The disciple whom Jesus loved, perhaps John himself, is on Jesus' right, and is able to lean back against Jesus and ask who he means. (This place on the host's right was given to his chief helper in putting on the meal.) The camera moves along the table. Jesus takes a piece of bread, dips it into the dish, leans back in turn and passes it to Judas, who is on his immediate left. It is easy for them to speak without the others hearing or understanding what is going on. On Jesus' left – did you note its significance? It is the place of honour, the place literally of the bosom friend, the one to whom the bread might fittingly be given as a mark of respect, as Boaz did to Ruth, in another seminal story of loyalty and love. John's account of the Last Supper has only this 'bread of the sop', not the breaking of bread that became our Communion, but the contrast was surely in John's mind. We are one bread, one body – how terrible when one who takes the bread is the betrayer.

QUESTION

Who are you close to that you are actually not close to?
What should you be doing about that?

Feeling the Cold

The words of the Psalm must have been in Jesus' thoughts. 'Even my close friend, whom I trusted, he who shared my bread, has lifted up his heel against me … If an enemy were insulting me, I could endure it; if a foe were raising himself against me, I could hide from him. But it is you, a man like myself, my companion, my close friend, with whom I once enjoyed sweet fellowship as we walked with the throng at the house of God.' *(Psalm 41:9 ff)*

There have been many attempts to understand Judas. Perhaps the most convincing is that he was a zealot, a dagger-man – *Iscariot* – who thought that Jesus would lead a great rebellion and, dismayed by his acceptance of the cross as his glory, sought to provoke not his arrest but his violent triumph over arrest and the outbreak of the uprising.

This is modern thinking, though, and not at all how John sees it. For him it is a matter of pure evil. Satan enters the Iscariot. Shakespeare borrows this moment for the turning point of his own drama of willing open-ness to evil: 'What you are about to do, do quickly,' says Jesus. 'If it were done when 'tis done,' says Macbeth, 'then 'twere well it were done quickly*.' Macbeth and Judas alike choose to be creatures of the dark. 'As soon as Judas had taken the bread he went out. And it was night.' It is the antithesis of Nicodemus who came by night to see Jesus. Judas leaves him by night, and as the camera looks out through the open door we can almost feel the cold.

All my enemies whisper together against me; they imagine the worst for me, saying, 'A vile disease has beset him; he will never get up from the place where he lies.'

Even my close friend, whom I trusted, he who shared my bread, has lifted up his heel against me.

But you, O LORD, have mercy on me; raise me up, that I may repay them. I know that you are pleased with me, for my enemy does not triumph over me. In my integrity you uphold me and set me in your presence forever.

Praise be to the LORD, the God of Israel, from everlasting to everlasting.

Amen and Amen.

PSALM 41.7-END

QUESTION

Is there evil to be resisted in your life?
What steps can you take to do that?

My Solemn Vow

Loyalty and betrayal: the immortal themes of the love story. Love and loyalty, love and marriage 'go together like a horse and carriage.' Preparing couples for their weddings, I look for every opportunity to help them understand that it is the unconditional acceptance of and commitment to the other that is at the heart of marriage, which makes marriage unlike any other relationship – and which makes its renunciation in divorce such a shattering blow.

I, N, take thee, N, to my wedded husband, to have and to hold from this day forward, for better for worse, for richer for poorer, in sickness and in health, to love and to cherish, till death us do part, according to God's holy ordinance; and thereto I plight thee my troth.

BOOK OF COMMON PRAYER
Marriage Service

Loyalty in another mode is the glue that bonds the brigade, the regiment together. Loyalty is what was turned on its head in Saddam Hussein's regime of terror in Iraq. The Republican Guard were offered better bread one day, to keep them loyal, and the threat of a bullet the next, to keep them loyal. Loyalty worth the name is always and entirely voluntary: love freely given in full knowledge of the cost and consequence. It was the nails, goes the old saying, that held Christ to the Cross, but his love that bound him there. Joseph Trapp wrote some rather naughty verses on a less than free loyalty when George I gave the late Bishop of Ely's library to Whig Cambridge rather than Tory Oxford. You need to remember that 'wanting' means 'lacking':

> The King, observing with judicious eyes
> The state of both his universities,
> To Oxford sent a troop of horse, and why?
> That learned body wanted loyalty;
> To Cambridge books, as very well discerning
> How much that loyal body wanted learning*.

QUESTION

How can you be more loyal? What does loyalty mean in your family relationships? At work? At church?

22

One Bread, One Body

Loyalty is there again in the dying art of the family gathered round the meal table and not dispersed each to their own room – a possibility opened up by the distributed warmth that we misleadingly call central heating, so unlike the hearth, the *focus* as the Latins called it, around which family grew. One for all and all for one becomes one by one, each all in all to themselves. When one of our family members storms off from the meal table the hurt can be excruciating, but to have no table to storm from is the death of family.

Hearth and table: it makes me think of bread, and if we were together I would invite you to share with me some that we (well, my wife Jean!) often bake, to break off a piece and eat it. It is a sort of bread called Chollah, used at the Jewish Kiddush meal.

Bread is the very symbol of shared life and community. The word *Lady* originally meant the bread-kneader in Anglo-Saxon, and *Lord* its guardian, the loaf-ward. Supermarkets have learned the value of having bakeries in-store, and pipe the bread-scented air to the door to welcome us. In our families and in our congregations we are one bread, one body.

QUESTION

Check out your own meal-time patterns and behaviour. Are you building family, the body?

Or are We?

That goes clean against the way of today's world, perhaps of any world. As I typed 'We are one bread, one body' into my word processor, its program complained. 'Error in number agreement' flashed up on the screen. We in the way of the world cannot be one. We are many. But this is the church, the body of Christ, not the world. We are one, one bread, one body.

Love bade me welcome; yet my soul drew back,
    Guilty of dust and sin.
But quick-eyed Love, observing me grow slack
    From my first entrance in,
Drew nearer to me, sweetly questioning,
    If I lack'd any thing.

'A guest', I answer'd, 'worthy to be here.'
    Love said, 'You shall be he.'
'I the unkind, ungrateful? Ah, my dear,
    I cannot look on thee.'
Love took my hand, and smiling did reply,
    'Who made the eyes but I?'

'Truth, Lord, but I have marr'd them: let my shame
    Go where it doth deserve.'
'And know you not,' says Love, 'who bore the blame?'
    'My dear, then I will serve.'
'You must sit down,' says Love, 'and taste my meat.'
    So I did sit and eat.

GEORGE HERBERT*

Or are we? Judas and Macbeth were hardly suspected until it was too late. It is characteristic of the darkness that it wears innocence as a mask. Until it is too late. As a matter of pure statistics, some of you reading this booklet could well be cheating on a marriage, breaking up a family, running down a fellow church member, mixing your outward religious observance with the heady world of drugs and dishonesty, sin and strange beliefs that are as much part of our world as they were of Jesus' and John's. It could so easily, so very easily, be any one of us, from bishop to bartender, from pastor to postman.

When you next take the bread at the Lord's table, when you next share the body of Christ, let sin leave by the door, while you do sit and eat.

It's true. I admit it.
I can't go on pretending.
I'm a mess.
Actually, it's a relief to come clean.
I can't think how much I've invested
In keeping up appearances.
So what am I going to do now, Lord?
Self-pity sounds attractive.
But you want to take
Even that out of my hands.
Ouch!
You want me not just to own up
But to give up,
Even grow up.
This isn't going to be easy, Lord.
I think I'm addicted to my self, my sin,
My in-my-own-shell-ness.
But when I say 'me',
You say, 'We.'

Christ has no body now on earth but yours,
no hands but yours, no feet but yours;
yours are the eyes through which he is to look
with compassion on the world;
yours are the feet with which he is to go about doing good;
and yours the hands with which he is to bless us now.
Amen.

St Teresa of Avila*

THURSDAY
Farewells: The Time Has Come

Today's Bible passage

It was just before the Passover Feast. Jesus knew that the time had come for him to leave this world and go to the Father. Having loved his own who were in the world, he now showed them the full extent of his love.

The evening meal was being served, and the devil had already prompted Judas Iscariot, son of Simon, to betray Jesus. Jesus knew that the Father had put all things under his power, and that he had come from God and was returning to God; so he got up from the meal, took off his outer clothing, and wrapped a towel round his waist. After that, he poured water into a basin and began to wash his disciples' feet, drying them with the towel that was wrapped round him.

He came to Simon Peter, who said to him, 'Lord, are you going to wash my feet?'

Jesus replied, 'You do not realise now what I am doing, but later you will understand.'

'No,' said Peter, 'you shall never wash my feet.'

Jesus answered, 'Unless I wash you, you have no part with me.'

'Then, Lord,' Simon Peter replied, 'not just my feet but my hands and my head as well!'

Jesus answered, 'A person who has had a bath needs only to wash his feet; his whole body is clean. And you are clean, though not every one of you.' For he knew who was going to betray him, and that was why he said not every one was clean.

When he had finished washing their feet, he put on his clothes and returned to his place. 'Do you understand what I have done for you?' he asked them. 'You call me "Teacher" and "Lord", and rightly so, for that is what I am. Now that I, your Lord and Teacher, have washed your feet, you also should wash one another's feet. I have set you an example that you should do as I have done for you. I tell you the truth, no servant is greater than his master, nor is a messenger greater than the one who sent him. Now that you know these things, you will be blessed if you do them.

'Now is the Son of Man glorified and God is glorified in him. If God is glorified in him, God will glorify the Son in himself, and will glorify him at once.

'My children, I will be with you only a little longer. You will look for me, and just as I told the Jews, so I tell you now: Where I am going, you cannot come.

'A new command I give you: Love one another. As I have loved you, so you must love one another. By this all men will know that you are my disciples, if you love one another.'

JOHN 13.1-17, 31b-35

Making a Point

Have you ever done something, not because it needed doing, but to make a point? I suppose the iconic scene of the crowd and troops pulling down the great statue of Saddam Hussein in Baghdad's Paradise Square falls into that category. They did it because the action captured more powerfully than words ever could the feeling of the moment. The television footage will be replayed for as long as there are TV sets to play it.

It was rather like that for Jesus at the Last Supper. He knows that events are reaching a crisis. He knows that in a few short hours he will be living out the full extent of God's love. He knows too that betrayal, fear, sheer humanity will make it hard for his disciples to stay with him, to understand what it all means. So he washes his disciples' feet just as the food arrives, as a sign of love.

The sound of chatter fades into the background as we track his actions. He lays down his outer clothing, and takes up the towel – just as he will shortly lay down his life and take it up again from the dead. Slowly the disciples turn to look at what is going on. Conversation stops. We hear the noise of the water being poured out, and our viewpoint moves with that of Jesus, looking down at each pair of feet, up at each bewildered face.

QUESTION

Imagine you are waiting at table at the Last Supper.
How do you react to the foot-washing?

A New Commandment

As always it is Peter who breaks the silence with his spluttered question. The pronouns in the Greek are packed emphatically into its beginning: '*You*, Lord, *my* feet to wash?' Just as Peter found it difficult to accept what Jesus' Messiahship meant, he finds it difficult to accept what Jesus' love is. Those of you who know Ford Madox Brown's painting of the foot-washing will remember what a grimace Peter gives!

Yet the foot-washing is precisely a sign of love. There is a crucial lesson to be taught and learnt. 'A new command I give you: Love one another. As I have loved you, so you must love one another. By this all men will know that you are my disciples, if you love one another.'

QUESTION

What does 'love', that slippery word, mean for you, now?

The Ladder of Love

All this talk of love, not to mention washing feet, must I think have been as awkward and embarrassing then as it is now. It can help to bring some reflection and analysis to bear on the subject so that we have some sort of bridge between this rather alien 'then' and our very challenging 'now'.

One of the great writers on love in the Middle Ages was Bernard of Clairvaux*, who combined sound learning with a mystic's desire for God. In his treatise *On Loving God* he builds a sort of

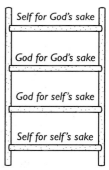

Self for God's sake

God for God's sake

God for self's sake

Self for self's sake

The Ladder of Love
Bernard of Clairvaux

ladder of love. First comes the love of self for self's sake. From this we rise to the love of God, but still for self's sake, and then to the love of God for God's own sake. Finally, and with a wonderful twist, we return to the love of self, but now not for self's sake, but for God's. The ladder charts our progress from selfishness and self-absorption, to our co-opting of God and religion to meet our needs, to the worship of God just for who he is, to the simple acceptance of self, with all our needs, because we are beloved of God.

We can look at foot-washing in the same way. I can wash my own feet for my own sake. I often do. I can wash your feet for my sake: they really are rather smelly I'm afraid. I can wash your feet for your own sake: perhaps you are past being able to reach down to them. And finally, I can wash my feet for your sake – when I realise that my feet are getting up your nose even more than yours are getting up mine!

Or again we can see the ladder at work in, say, Peter's desire always to be doing. We start with what we can do for ourselves; then to what God can do for us; then what we can do for God (the classic Anglo-Saxon attitude); and finally what God can do through us – the attitude of Jesus.

What these ladders do is mark out the cliffs which we must climb if we are to grow in love – a struggle which begins by leaving behind self, and which ends by re-discovering it; a journey whose progress is measured by the extent to which our self is transformed by the presence of God within us.

QUESTION

Do you find the 'ladder of love' helpful? Where do you fit?

'Up Close and Personal'

This involves intimacy. As I was writing this my wife reminded me of a time in Banbury when we were being visited regularly by gentlemen of the road en route from Oxford to Stratford. One man arrived looking even more desperate than usual, haggard, with long unkempt black hair and beard, stinking to high heaven. The smell came from his feet which were in an awful state, and he asked for new socks. Jean remembered that I had a spare pair of hiking ones, but knew that it was not enough simply to hand them over: she would have to help him put them on.

Slowly she peeled off his shoes and the old socks that had grown into the skin, and washed his feet. It became clear that he needed urgent medical attention, so we took him to the Oxford hostel he was making for: I have to tell you that Jean is no saint, but I don't think I could have done what she did then. What about you?

Intimacy … Think of your own towel at home. It matters who you share your towel with. We can take it as an icon of the deeper question, who are we prepared to share our real selves with?

QUESTION

Who do you share with deeply?
(And who are you avoiding that needs you?)

Behind the Façade

One of the more interesting aspects of a job which involves meeting a lot of people, with some licence to be involved with them, is considering just what those people are like behind the façade they present to the world. I remember watching Debenham's (formerly Elliston and Cavell's) in Oxford being rebuilt a few years ago now. The Victorian front was carefully propped up with scaffolding, while the rabbit warren behind it was completely demolished, and a whole new steel and concrete structure erected in its place. A photograph 'before and after' would show scarcely a difference from the outside, but inside …

Most of us are rather like that store. What is it that makes our public face so important to us – and our private being so tender? Why are close friendship and intimacy both so desirable, and so daunting? One clue from our 'ladder of love' is to note that we start from a heavily defended position by nature, it seems. Older theologians would call it a consequence of the Fall, the same need for a fig-leaf that we see after the apple has been eaten. We are self-conscious, unsure of ourselves – and very often those who seem least like this are in fact the best examples of it. It is remarkable that in an age when we have living standards and social achievements undreamt of even by our grand-parents, low self-esteem seems more prevalent a problem than ever.

To make progress, up the ladder, in our lives, we need to dare to share: share something of our real selves with another, whatever name we give them. Without that there is every likelihood that our spiritual journey will be stalled; and a significant danger too that in our personal relationships some of the unexploded canister shot of life will blow us apart.

One of our children, when asked by us to be a victim (I mean volunteer!) for the annual foot-washing ceremony on Maundy

Thursday at the cathedral, said quickly and loudly, 'They're my feet!' Indeed. That is precisely the issue. Let me invite you today, whether literally or figuratively, to let someone be a 'foot-washer' for you, lest the walk of your life goes awry.

'How r u?' we ask these days
From the safe distance of a mobile phone.
'Fine,' I always say.
But I lie. '
I don't want to lie now, Lord, to you.
There's more than feet need washing
As far as I'm concerned.
A whole cupboardful of dirty linen,
Stained in the most embarrassing places.
I hope your life laundry
Lives up to expectations.
Ah.
I thought we'd be alone, Lord,
Just you and me, you know.
And now I gather that
Some of this laundering
Happens in
Company.
Amen.

Most merciful Lord,
your love compels us to come in.
Our hands were unclean,
our hearts were unprepared;
we were not fit
even to eat the crumbs from under your table.
But you, Lord, are the God of our salvation,
and share your bread with sinners.
So cleanse and feed us
with the precious body and blood of your Son,
that he may live in us and we in him;
and that we, with the whole company of Christ,
may sit and eat in your kingdom.
Amen.

ALTERNATIVE SERVICE BOOK, *Alternative Prayer of Humble Access**

Crisis: Here is the Man!

Today's Bible passage

Simon Peter and another disciple were following Jesus. Because this disciple was known to the high priest, he went with Jesus into the high priest's courtyard, but Peter had to wait outside at the door. The other disciple, who was known to the high priest, came back, spoke to the girl on duty there and brought Peter in.

'You are not one of his disciples, are you?' the girl at the door asked Peter.

He replied, 'I am not.'

It was cold, and the servants and officials stood round a fire they had made to keep warm. Peter also was standing with them, warming himself.

Meanwhile, the high priest questioned Jesus about his disciples and his teaching.

'I have spoken openly to the world,' Jesus replied. 'I always taught in synagogues or at the temple, where all the Jews come together. I said nothing in secret. Why question me? Ask those who heard me. Surely they know what I said.'

When Jesus said this, one of the officials near by struck him in the face. 'Is this the way you answer the high priest?' he demanded.

'If I said something wrong,' Jesus replied, 'testify as to what is wrong. But if I spoke the truth, why did you strike me?' Then Annas sent him, still bound, to Caiaphas the high priest.

As Simon Peter stood warming himself, he was asked, 'You are not one of his disciples, are you?'

He denied it, saying, 'I am not.'

One of the high priest's servants, a relative of the man whose ear Peter had cut off, challenged him, 'Didn't I see you with him in the olive grove?' Again Peter denied it, and at that moment a cock began to crow.

Then the Jews led Jesus from Caiaphas to the palace of the Roman governor. By now it was early morning, and to avoid ceremonial uncleanness the Jews did not enter the palace; they wanted to be able to eat the Passover. So Pilate came out to them and asked, 'What charges are you bringing against this man?'

'If he were not a criminal,' they replied, 'we would not have handed him over to you.' Pilate said, 'Take him yourselves and judge him by your own law.'

'But we have no right to execute anyone,' the Jews objected. This happened so that the words Jesus had spoken indicating the kind of death he was going to die would be fulfilled.

Pilate then went back inside the palace, summoned Jesus and asked him, 'Are you the king of the Jews?'

'Is that your own idea,' Jesus asked, 'or did others talk to you about me?'

'Am I a Jew?' Pilate replied. 'It was your people and your chief priests who handed you over to me. What is it you have done?'

Jesus said, 'My kingdom is not of this world. If it were, my servants would fight to prevent my arrest by the Jews. But now my kingdom is from another place.'

'You are a king, then!' said Pilate.

Jesus answered, 'You are right in saying I am a king. In fact, for this reason I was born, and for this I came into the world, to testify to the truth. Everyone on the side of truth listens to me.'

'What is truth?' Pilate asked. With this he went out again to the Jews and said, 'I find no basis for a charge against him. But it is your custom for me to release to you one prisoner at the time of the Passover. Do you want me to release "the king of the Jews"?'

They shouted back, 'No, not him! Give us Barabbas!' Now Barabbas had taken part in a rebellion.

Then Pilate took Jesus and had him flogged. The soldiers twisted together a crown of thorns and put it on his head. They clothed him in a purple robe and went up to him again and again, saying, 'Hail, king of the Jews!' And they struck him in the face.

Once more Pilate came out and said to the Jews, 'Look, I am bringing him out to you to let you know that I find no basis for a charge against him.' When Jesus came out wearing the crown of thorns and the purple robe, Pilate said to them, 'Here is the man!'

JOHN 18:15-19.5

Behold the Man!

Can you remember the moment when you first realised that the 'lamb' you were eating for Sunday dinner was the same sort of 'lamb' that had melted your heart as it cavorted so innocently in the field nearby?

'Behold,' says the Baptist at the beginning of John's Gospel, 'Behold the Lamb of God that takes away the sins of the world.' For John, it is Good Friday not Maundy Thursday that is the day of the Passover, and Jesus is the lamb of the sacrifice. The Man we behold is also the Lamb.

A statue stood for a while in Trafalgar Square, a few years ago now*. Formed in some white marble-like material, it showed a young man, naked but for a loin-cloth, standing calm and serene. On his head was a crown of thorns. Most passers by were confused, annoyed, even angry. It was Christ, but not Christ. It showed this same scene of Pilate's mocking presentation of Jesus to the crowd – 'Behold, the man' – but there was no sense of disturbance on his face.

It was in fact, wittingly or unwittingly, a portrayal of Christ which is remarkably true to St John's Gospel. When the soldiers come to arrest Jesus, John uses language which implies a massive overkill: the word for the soldier's detachment implies a thousand men. But neither are the troops needed, nor does Jesus wait for Judas to betray him with a kiss. He, 'knowing all that was going to happen to him, went out and asked them, "Who is it you want?"' The issue is not in doubt.

QUESTION

Ponder the power of innocence.
*Are you – like Judas – wanting Jesus to **do** something?*

Disclosure

Around this still centre, the other characters in the drama break like waves against a cliff and are revealed for what they are. The accusers of Jesus find themselves appealing to the very Roman authority that they regarded as illegitimate in order to gain a conviction: 'We have no king but Caesar!' Their internal divisions will soon see Jerusalem razed to the ground by another Caesar. Pilate the judge gives the order for Jesus' destruction,

but while Jesus rises from the dead, Pilate will over-reach himself and be called to Rome to face death himself. Giotto's painting of Pilate captures both the power and the vulnerability*. Look at the eyes. Look at the mouth and chin.

John's whole passion is full of this irony and double story. When Caiaphas says that it is better for one man to die than the whole people to perish, John points up the two-fold meaning: the practical plot to abort an uprising which would spell Roman retribution and the priests' own downfall, and the prophetic insight of the high priest unwittingly declaring the very heart of the gospel.

QUESTION

Are you finding things out about yourself as you come up against the Passion of Christ?

I am the Truth

Or take Pilate's superscription on the cross of Christ: 'Jesus of Nazareth, the King of the Jews.' 'What I have written, I have written,' he says, when challenged by the chief priests. But is it mockery, or the truth? Indeed, 'What is truth?' is found on Pilate's own lips, while the drama of John's passion points us inexorably towards the calm figure at the still centre of its action – Christ who is the truth, the way and the life. No one comes to the Father except through him.

So we behold the man. I suggested a moment ago that the words were said in mockery. Or are they another declaration of truth? Look, here is true humanity. Here is one who is simply man as he was meant to be. Here is one who is simply himself without need of mask or clothes. Here is one who does not mould himself against others, but is the mould against which they are measured.

Spirit of the living God
fall afresh on me;
Spirit of the living God
fall afresh on me;
break me, melt me,
mould me, fill me;
Spirit of the living God
fall afresh on me.

DANIEL IVERSON*

QUESTION

Is Christ calling you to be moulded more truly by and against him? Are the words of the song comforting or challenging for you?

The One who Is

Philip Larkin, the poet, described religion as 'that vast, moth-eaten musical brocade / created to pretend we never die.*' Leading worship regularly at a cathedral now – we have our foibles – I can see what he means. But here the diced-for garment of Jesus, woven in one piece, displays a simplicity and honesty that betrays the similarly seamless garments of the high priest. Religion then and now can lose its way, but at the heart of the gospel stands not the vain repetition of religion, but a single, very real, historical man, who simply IS.

John's Gospel is famous for its 'I am' sayings. 'I am the Bread of Life.' 'I am the Vine.' 'I am the Good Shepherd.' So Jesus' answer when the arresting soldiers say it is Jesus of Nazareth they seek is simply, 'I am.' Not 'I am he,' as our tidy translations have it. Just, 'I am.' The name of God. Again, before the high priest, that word 'I' is emphasised. 'I said nothing in secret. Why question me?'

Interleaved with these scenes are those of Peter in the courtyard. And what is his refrain? Not 'I am' but 'I am not.' 'You're not one of his disciples, are you?' 'I am not.' The actions indoors and out run alongside each other like the famous quartet scene at the dénouement of *Rigoletto*. As we cut from one to the other tension builds, until the cock begins to crow. Even Jesus' principal follower cannot stay with him. Jesus stands alone. He alone IS.

QUESTION

We are nearly at the end of our journey.
Are you ready to simply stay in the presence of Jesus
even when he is in the tomb, waiting for Easter?

Love is

As we have journeyed with John through this Holy Week, we have encountered a love that is generous to the point of extravagance, sacrificial to the point of death, commitedly loyal, necessarily intimate. There have been a lot of words. Back in the days of the Beatles there were Mersey Poets as well as the Mersey Sound, and they wrote about love more simply.

The poem I have in mind is by Adrian Henri*, called *Love is*.

Love is feeling cold in the back of vans
Love is a fanclub with only two fans
Love is walking holding paintstained hands
Love is

Love is fish and chips on winter nights
Love is blankets full of strange delights
Love is when you don't put out the lights
Love is

I think I'd better stop at that point, but the point is that each verse does stop – with 'Love is.' Not with another something that love is. Just, 'Love is.'

God is. That, at the end of theology, is what we mean by God. God is. God is love. Love is. We learn a very great deal about ourselves when the music stops, and when we simply have to be. We want to look away, read a book, hum a tune, start a conversation.

'Human kind cannot bear much reality. But at the still point of the turning world, there the dance is, but neither arrest nor movement.

If you came this way taking any route, starting from anywhere, at any time or season, it would always be the same: you would have to put off sense and notion. You are not here to verify, instruct yourself, or inform curiosity or carry report. You are here to kneel, where prayer has been valid.*'

Poets are often better theologians than the clergy. As T.S. Eliot says – it was his words from *Four Quartets* that I was quoting just now – you and I are here to kneel, before the cross, where prayer has been valid, where prayer may be valid now. We look at the cross and see the still body of Christ, the still centre of this turning world. But this is no stillness of death, or not only the stillness of death. Heaven is holding its breath, in that moment when the dance is, but there is no movement or sound, only the truth of the dance, waiting for the dance to live in us. Our task is to enter the silence, and the joining of the silence of earth with the silence of heaven is what we call prayer.

You've gone.
Just when we'd got something going.
Just when I thought I'd found somebody
Who could really understand.
Why don't you do something?
If you are the Son of God –
Oh dear.
I seem to remember
Those words
From somewhere else.
Lead me, Lord, not into temptation,
But deliver me from evil.

Jesus, Lord,
Still on the cross
For love of human kind:
Draw me still to you,
And in the stillness
Save me.
Amen.

Christ crucified draw you to himself,
to find in him a sure ground for faith,
a firm support for hope,
and the assurance of sins forgiven;
and the blessing of God Almighty,
Father, Son and Holy Spirit,
be upon you,
and remain with you always.
Amen.

COMMON PRAYER, *Passiontide Blessing* *

REFERENCES by page number

6 The saying is sometimes attributed to Augustine but not with any security. Richard Burridge cites it at the beginning of his *John, The People's Bible Commentary* (BRF, Oxford 1998) p.12.

8 W. H. Vanstone's poem is found at the end of his book *Love's Endeavour, Love's Expense* (DLT, London 1977) p.119.

8 You can find Newman's hymn in most standard hymnbooks – such as *Complete Mission Praise* 563 and *Common Praise* 557.

9 John Boyle O'Reilly (1844-1890) from *In Bohemia*, st. 5 (1886).

9 For Bob Thompson's story, see e.g. http://www.beysterinstitute.org/onlinemag/oct99/briefcase.html

11 St Richard was bishop of Chichester in the thirteenth century.

13 Josephus, *Jewish Wars 6, 9, 3*.

15 For Shannon Wright and the Jonesboro killings see e.g. http://www.case-studies.com/articles/jonesboro_bullet.html

16 For St Alphege see e.g. http://www.britannia.com/bios/abofc/aelfheah.html

16 For Elizabeth of Hungary see e.g. F.L. Cross, *The Oxford Dictionary of the Christian Church*, 3rd edition ed. E.A. Livingstone (OUP, Oxford 1997) p. 540.

16 For Edith Cavell see e.g. http://www.edithcavell.org.uk.

16 For Janani Luwum see A. Chandler (ed.), *The Terrible Alternative* (Cassell, London 1998) pp. 144-158.

21 William Shakespeare, *Macbeth*, Act 1, scene 7

22 Joseph Trapp (1679-1747) *On George I's Donation of the Bishop of Ely's Library to Cambridge University*.

24 George Herbert (1593-1633), *Love* reprinted in *The New Oxford Book of Christian Verse* ed. D. Davie (OUP, Oxford 1981) p.81.

25 For St Teresa of Avila (1515-1582), see e.g. *ODCC* p.1589.

28 St Bernard of Clairvaux's treatise, written c.1126, is printed in translation in *The Twelve Steps of Humility and Loving God*, ed. H. C. Backhouse (Hodder and Stoughton, London 1985).

31 *The Alternative Service Book 1980* (CUP, Cambridge 1980) p.170.

34 The statue *Ecce Homo* is by Mark Wallinger. See e.g. the news report at http://news.bbc.co.uk/1/hi/uk/399711.stm

35 For the life of Giotto di Bondone (c.1267-1337) see *ODCC* p. 678. The painting of Pilate is in the corner of the fresco depicting the mocking of Jesus by the Temple guards in the Cappella degli Scrovegni at Padua (1305).

36 Iverson's song is in most standard songbooks e.g. *Complete Mission Praise* 613.

36 From Philip Larkin's *Aubade* (Charles Seluzicki, 1980).

37 From Adrian Henri, *Love Is …* in *Penguin Modern Poets 10* rev. & enlgd. ed. (Penguin, Harmondsworth 1967) p.21.

38 T.S. Eliot, *Four Quartets*, 'Little Gidding' in *The Complete Poems and Plays of T.S. Eliot* (Faber and Faber, London 1969) p.192.

39 From *Common Worship: Service and Prayers for the Church of England* (Church House Publishing, London 2000) p.313

Photo Credits

Cover The Ivegill lectern at Carlisle Cathedral, with thanks to James Armstrong.

16 *Statue of Bishop Luwum* by kind permission of the Dean and Chapter of Westminster.

34 With thanks to St Martins-in-the-Fields Church, London.

The use of all copyright material quoted in this book is gratefully acknowledged.